Picture credits:
l: Left, r: Right, t: Top, b: Bottom, c: Centre

Cover images: background: Tomasz Otap/Shutterstock, tl, tr: jamesbenet/Istockphoto,
mr: Colman Lerner Gerardo/Shutterstock, bc: Tom Werner/Shutterstock, br: Shawn Kretz/Istockphoto
Backcover: bl: Gene Lee/Shutterstock, br: Olga Gabay/Shutterstock.

17t: Scott Leigh/Istockphoto, 17m: Jamesbenet/Istockphoto, 17b: Kristen Johansen/Istockphoto,
19b: Timothy Livingston/Istockphoto, 21t: Gordon Galbraith/Shutterstock, 22b: NorthGeorgiaMedia/Shutterstock,
23t: Jiri Vatka/Istockphoto, 29b: Library of Congress, 31b: Tomasz Otap/Shutterstock,
32t: Jamesbenet/Istockphoto, 37t: Mlenny/Istockphoto, 37b: Shawn Kretz/Istockphoto,
40b: Elias H. Debbas II/Shutterstock.

Published By: Robert Frederick Ltd.
4 North Parade Bath, England.

First Published: 2007

Designed and packaged by
Q2A MEDIA
Printed in China.

Discover the Aztecs

CONTENTS

Who Were They?

We, the Aztecs, spent hundreds of years travelling from place to place, till our god told us to settle down on an island in your modern Mexico City. Then we expanded our empire and ruled most parts of modern Mexico. This is the reason why we are also known as Mexicas.

The Starting Point

The Aztecs were a Native American tribe who lived in Central America from the 14th to the 16th century. The Aztecs had a well-developed culture and boasted of many great achievements. They were a pragmatic and educated race and showed their skills in administration, architecture and farming. From being a nomadic tribe, that moved from place to place, they went on to create a huge empire. The empire started with the discovery of the city of Tenochtitlan on Lake Texcoco in 1325. It was from then that this race became more and more powerful. At first they made alliances with their neighbours to gain control over surrounding lands. But soon they began taking over the lands by force and by the 16th century they controlled large parts of northern Mexico. However, their rich and successful empire collapsed when the Spaniards attacked and destroyed Tenochtitlan in 1521.

This is what an Aztec man looked like in those days

Would you believe?

The areas marked in pink show the extent of the Aztec empire at its height. The Aztecs ruled over most parts of Mexico except the small areas marked in orange.

Important Rulers

We had several good rulers who helped us expand our empire. A council of noble elders chose eligible sons of the kings as successors to the throne.

Aztec Rulers

Acamapichtli 1376–1396

- SON: **Huitzilihuitl** 1397–1417
  - SON: **Itzcoatl** 1428–1440
  - SON: **Moctezuma Ilhuicamina** 1440–1469
    - DAUGHTER
- SON: **Chimalpopoca** 1417–1427
  - SON

Chimalpopoca's son and Moctezuma Ilhuicamina's daughter married and had three sons.

- SON: **Axayacatl** 1469–1481
  - SON: **Moctezuma Xocoyotzin** 1502–1520
  - SON: **Cuitlahuac** 1520
- SON: **Tizoc** 1481–1486
- SON: **Ahuitzotl** 1486–1502
  - SON: **Cuauhtemoc** 1520–1525

Moctezuma II wore a gold crown topped with 400 bright feathers

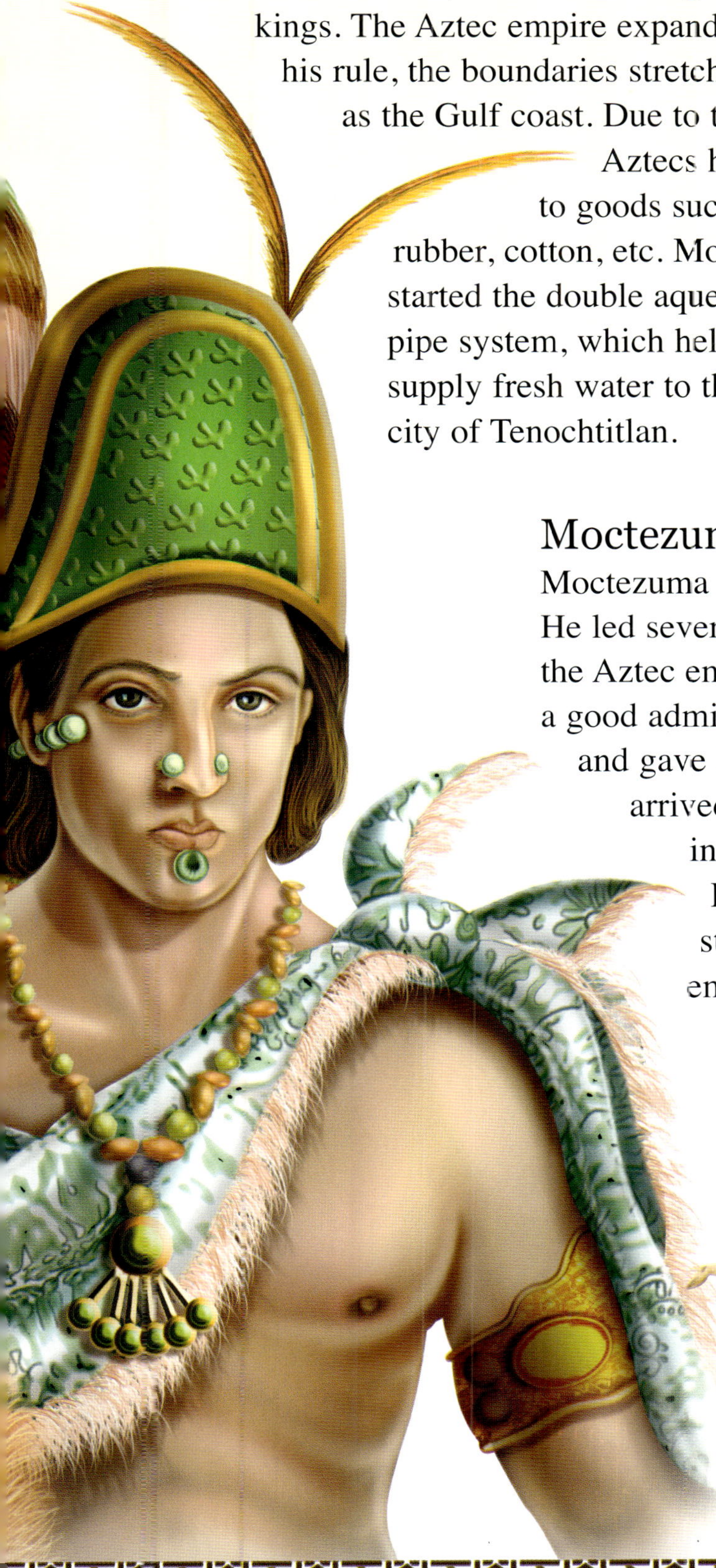

Moctezuma I

Moctezuma Ilhuicamina, also called Moctezuma I, was one of the greatest Aztec kings. The Aztec empire expanded under his rule, the boundaries stretching as far as the Gulf coast. Due to this the Aztecs had access to goods such as cocoa, rubber, cotton, etc. Moctezuma started the double aqueduct pipe system, which helped supply fresh water to the city of Tenochtitlan.

Moctezuma I defeated the Mixtecs of Coixtlahuaca in 1458

Moctezuma II

Moctezuma Xocoyotzin was the last great Aztec king. He led several successful military campaigns and took the Aztec empire to its greatest glory. Moctezuma II was a good administrator. He created a rich and lavish court and gave it a semi-divine status. When the Spaniards arrived, Moctezuma II failed to realize their true intentions. He was captured in his own kingdom. He lost popularity with his people and they stoned him. He died soon after. The Aztec empire collapsed after his death.

Would you believe?

In 1428, Itzcoatl formed the Triple Alliance of the three Aztec city-states, of Tenochtitlán, Texcoco and Tlacopán. These city-states jointly ruled the area in and around the Valley of Mexico for the next 100 years. Tenochtitlán was the dominant partner.

Aztec Society

Our society was divided into three main classes: the nobility, commoners and slaves. People belonging to each class were involved in some specific work and their position in society depended on their class.

The Nobility

The nobility constituted of those who were highest in the social rank. It included people who were nobles by birth, priests and those who earned their rank. Among the nobility the highest social sphere was occupied by a minority of families known as the *pipiltin*. These people were members of the hereditary nobility and occupied the top positions in the government, the army and priesthood. The king, known as the *tlatoani* or "he that speaks" was elected by members of the nobility. The king was revered greatly and ruled until his death. Priests were also a highly respected group. They not only performed religious ceremonies but also acted as doctors and teachers. They also knew astronomy and astrology. Warriors too were an important part of the nobility.

The Commoners

The second class of people in the social structure were called the *macehualtin*. They were commoners, originally peasants, and included people engaged in agriculture and other common trades. The commoners worked the land in family units and kept their produce. However, the land was not owned by an individual alone, but collectively by inhabitants of the neighbourhood or the *calpulli*. Artisans and traders constituted more than half the *macehualtin* population. They were engaged in making and selling products. The serfs or the tenant farmers formed the lowest category of commoners. They were obliged to cultivate land owned by the nobility.

An Aztec noble was considered to be a very important person

The Slaves

The slaves, or the *tlacotin,* were common in the Aztec society. An Aztec could be made a slave as a punishment for non payment of debts, criminal acts or if he was captured during war. A poor father could sell his children as slaves and people could also sell themselves as slaves. But slavery in Aztec culture was very different from that in the European culture. For the Aztecs, slavery was not considered to be hereditary. So a slave's children were free. Slaves could also be set free if they were married to their masters or had children with their masters. Slaves were also allowed to buy property and possessions for themselves.The slaves could also buy their own freedom!

Slaves who earned a bad reputation had to wear a wooden collar attached with rings at the back of his neck

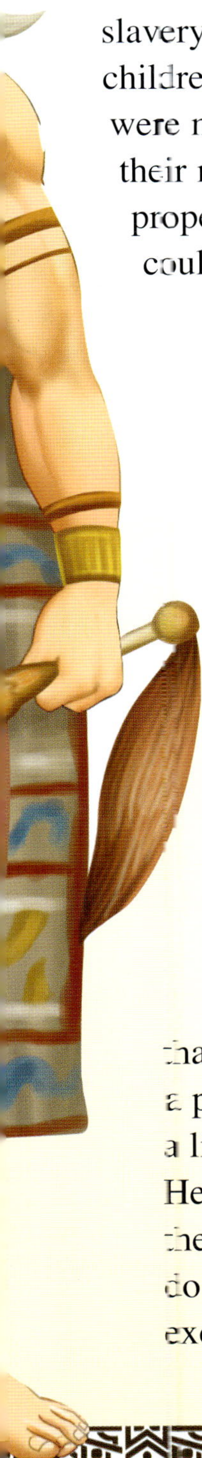

Moving Up

In the Aztec society the class system followed was rigid, with the nobility enjoying all the privileges and others enduring a hard life. However the Aztec class system was not completely stagnant. So it was possible for a commoner to rise up the social ladder and enjoy the life of a noble man. There were no walls separating the classes. The society did not work on the principal of hereditary succession alone. So if a peasant father had to struggle, it did not necessarily mean that his son would also have to be a peasant like his father and lead a life of hard work and drudgery. He could work towards moving up the social ladder. However to be able to do this, the commoner had to be exceptionally gifted and meritorious.

Would you believe?

Slaves were given one chance to escape before they were sold in the market. If the slave could escape from the market place and reach the sanctuary of the king's palace he became a free man! Everyone except the slave owner's son was forbidden to chase the slave.

How Were They Ruled?

We had quite systematic governance. The pipiltin ruled us well and we were happy with the administrative and legal systems.

Administration

The king was the supreme ruler in the Aztec society. He was the head of the law courts, priesthood and the army. Though he was greatly revered, his power was not absolute. He had to account for his deeds before those who chose him. The *tecuhtli* or the lords made up the ruling class. It comprised of administrators, warriors and judges. Each *tecuhtli* was responsible for a particular region and was considered the highest form of government in that region. In addition, each district or *calpulli* had a *calpullec* or the chieftain who was elected for life and was responsible for maintaining harmony within the community.

The diagram shows the different levels of social structure in the Aztec society

Legal System

The Aztecs had a very good legal system. There were lesser courts and a supreme judicial council. They had laws to deal with crimes, property ownership, marriage and also divorce. The offender for any crime was tried in a lesser court. Verdicts of the lesser court could be appealed for at a supreme judicial council. This council had to resolve appeals in 80 days. The king was the final judge and the council of judges had to consult him before deciding punishments. The Aztecs had harsh punishments for all criminals and capital punishment was also very common. Criminals were strangled, stoned and beaten to death. Confiscation of property, public humiliation and destruction of homes were other forms of punishment. At times restitution was common for minor thefts, frauds or personal injuries.

Would you believe?

The Aztec merchants were excluded from the codes of the Aztec legal system. They had their own system of justice for the market place as well as the criminal activities related to the merchant class.

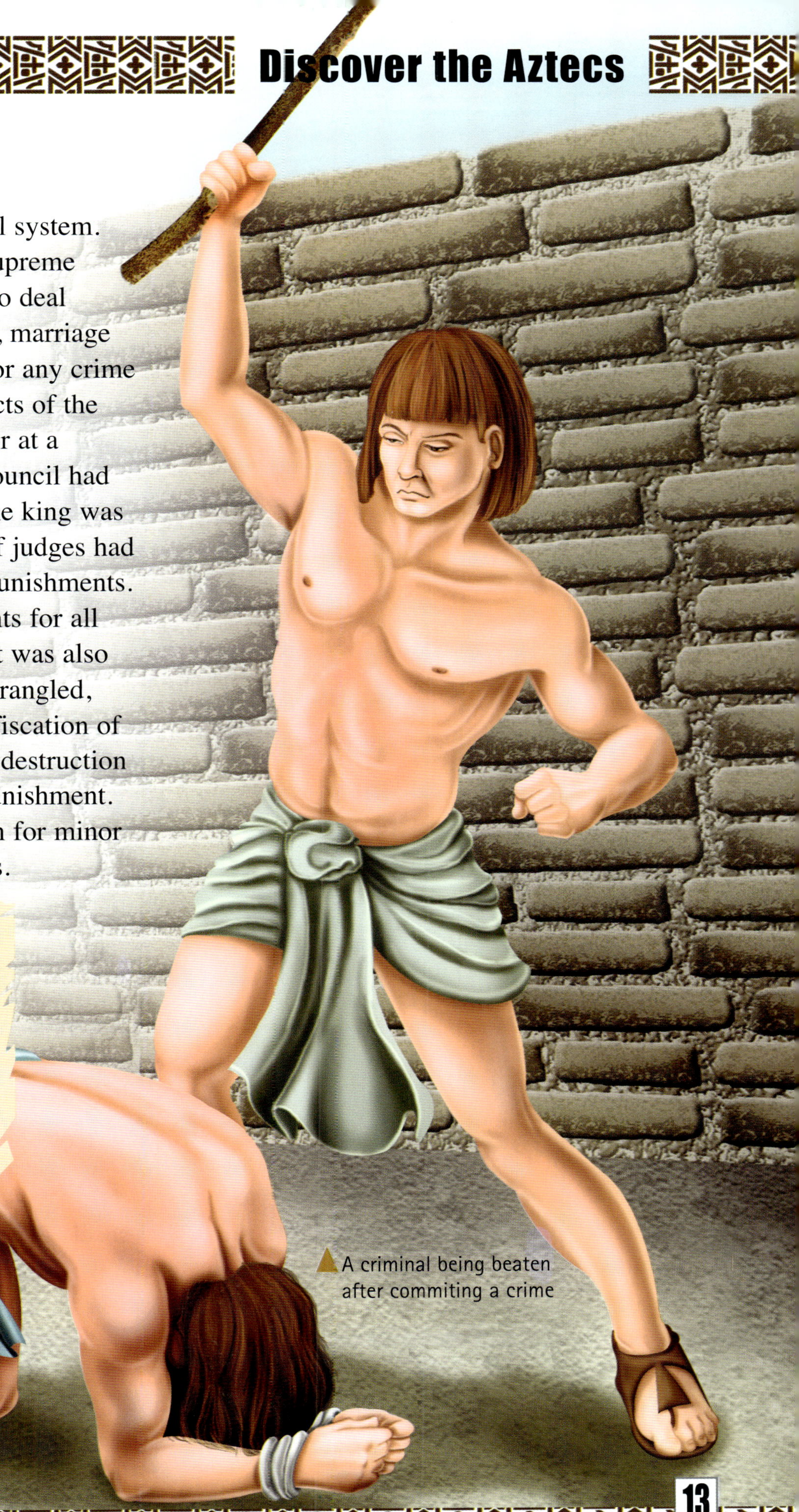

A criminal being beaten after commiting a crime

An Aztec family arranging the steam bath

Family Life

In our families men and women played distinct roles. Men sustained the family financially while the women took care of the home and children.

Home Sweet Home

The Aztec home had two buildings. One was the home and the other was the steam bath or the *temazca*l. The main home had walls of mud and a thatched roof. There was only one room - with a door but no windows. The room was divided into four areas - a kitchen area a dining area, a family shrine and a bedroom. The *temazca*l had a fire and chimney next to the bathing area. The heated walls of the stove heated the bathroom walls. Then water was poured on the walls to generate steam.

Marriage

Aztec men would get married between the age of 20 and 22. Women were married at 16. Marriage was a family affair in which the couple had little say. Soothsayers were called to check all the astrological details of the couple. Midwives mediated between two families to fix a marriage. It was only after marriage that Aztec men were officially considered a part of the society. Aztec men would have one legitimate wife and many secondary wives.

Children

As soon as a child was born, the midwife ensured that all sacred rites were performed. She named the baby and washed it with water while praying to Chalchiuhtlicue, the goddess of water. A soothsayer prepared the child's astrological chart. The child was baptized four days after birth. The midwife poured water drops on the baby's head and washed the baby's body. She would then lift the baby in her arms four times while invoking the blessings of the sun. Thus a child was introduced to Aztec custom right from birth.

Husband & Father / Wife & Mother

The man of the house worked and fought in battles and earned to sustain his family. The woman looked after the home and her family. The children were taught to follow their parents. The boys were trained to follow their father's trades and the daughters learnt to cook, clean, weave and to run a home.

Would you believe?

When an Aztec died, they were cremated. The exception to this rule was that those who died by drowning, were killed by lightning, had leprosy, or died while giving birth, were buried instead.

The wedding ceremony would be held at the groom's house a day after a feast at the bride's house

Farming and Food

Agriculture was an important part of our economy. In fact, we introduced crops such as corn and chilli peppers to Europe!

Floating Farms

The Aztecs did not have any farmland. So they had to create their own farmland on lakes. These were known as *chinampas*. Willow trees were planted on all sides of the *chinampa* because they grew quickly and the roots prevented the soil from being washed away. It was on these floating farms that the Aztecs grew their crops. The *chinampas* could be of any size. There was always enough space between one *chinampa* and another so that two canoes could pass between them. Aztec farmers travelled on canoes to till and harvest their crops.

Would you believe?

A large variety of insects - like grasshoppers, ants and worms - were a part of the Aztec diet. Insects were also harvested in large numbers. Aztecs were also fond of algae collected from the surface of the lakes.

The Aztecs built floating farms called chinampas by placing woven reed mats on the water. They were then surrounded by small fences

Our Crops, our Food

The mud that the Aztecs used to build the *chinampas* was rich in minerals and ideal for growing crops. They grew corn, tomatoes, potatoes, chilli peppers and squash on these floating farmlands. The roots of the plants grew to the bottom of the lake, getting an endless supply of water. In fact, corn, tomatoes, avocadoes and chilli peppers were carried back by Spanish explorers from the Aztec land. The Aztecs did not use ploughs or cattle to till the land. They just used a digging stick and a wooden hoe to grow and harvest crops.

Corn was an important part of the Aztec diet

The mortar and pestle were used by the Aztecs to grind spices used in their food

Chillies were used to flavour a kind of porridge called atolli. At times honey was also used

Yummy Meal

Corn and its flour were the staple diet of Aztecs. They also used maize to make *tortillas*. A kind of envelope made from steamed maize stuffed with vegetables, called *tamales*, was also a popular dish. Meat was reserved for the nobility. The flesh of dogs, turkeys and Musovy ducks were also eaten by the nobility, while the common people ate fish and seafood. A chocolate drink made from cacao mixed with powdered maize was also very popular. It was believed to provide stamina and was thus mainly drunk by warriors. The Aztecs had an alcoholic drink known as *octli*. It was made from the sap of the maguey plant.

Their Clothes

We mainly wore cotton clothes, well suited for the warm weather. Our clothes not only served to cover us but also helped to differentiate between different social classes.

Fabric Used

Most of the clothes the Aztecs wore were made from cotton dyed with vegetable dyes. They were also made from leaf fibres of various plants. Aztec women wove and spun the fibres to make cloth. This cloth was folded, tied and then used to make clothes for the family. Yards of cloth also served as tax payments to rulers. At times these were also sold in the market.

What They Wore

All Aztec men wore loincloths. Some of them also wore skirts. Most men wore a *tilmatli* which was a cape tied at the shoulder. All men carried a small pouch under their cloak to carry coca leaves to chew. They also carried amulets for good luck. Women wore a loose blouse and a long skirt wrapped around the waist. Clothing for the rich was made from cotton while the poor wore clothes made of maguey fibres.

This Aztec woman is weaving fibres that are then used to make clothes

Dress Right

Even though people wore similar style of clothes, it was easy to distinguish between a commoner and a noble by the clothes they wore. Nobles wore brightly coloured, patterned cotton clothes. The dress included symbols characteristic of their social rank. For example, bright feathers were used to adorn the dress worn by a noble. Priests tied their loincloth differently. The slaves were scantily dressed. There were rules about what the common people could wear, applying to shoes, hairstyles and jewellery. Nobles wore decorated leather sandals while commoners wore sandals made of woven leaves.

All Aztec men wore loincloths, while women wore a loose blouse with a skirt

Aztec nobles wore feathers on their head for various occassions

Would you believe?

The cloak, or *tilmatli*, of the Aztec men also served to distinguish their status . Upper class men wore cotton *tilmatli* tied over the right shoulder. The middle classes tied *tilmatli* made from maguey over their left shoulder. The serfs tied it behind the neck, and would use it for carrying things.

Gods and Myths

We worshipped over a thousand gods. We also had many interesting legends about them.

Head of the Gods

Huitzilopochtli was the Sun god and was also known as the God of War. He was the most celebrated of all deities. According to mythology, Huitzilopochtli was the son of Coatlicue or the Earth Goddess. When he was still in his mother's womb, his sister Coyolxauhqui schemed with other siblings and tried to kill him and their mother. Huitzilopochtli used bright rays to defeat her. It was Huitzilopochtli who told the Aztecs to wander till they found a place where there was an eagle, perched on a cactus, eating a snake.The Aztecs finally found the place, built a temple there and named the place Tenochtitlan.

Huitzilopochtli tossed his sister's head into the sky after defeating her

Tlaloc was depicted as a blue god with fangs

The God of Rain

Tlaloc was the god of rain and fertility. He was worshipped because farming was an important part of the Aztec economy. Moreover, it was believed that if angry, Tlaloc could unleash floods, lightning and drought. So children were sacrificed in his honour. The tears of the victims, seen to symbolise falling rain, were collected in a ceremonial bowl and offered to Tlaloc.

Quetzalcoatl's name meant 'feathered snake' and he was often worshipped in that form

The Father of Man

Quetzalcoatl was considered to be the Father of man. According to legends, Quetzalcoatl and his brother Xototl descended to hell to retrieve human bones. Then Quetzalcoatl dripped his blood into the bones and resurrected humans. He was a kind god who represented the arts, crafts and self sacrifice.

Would you believe?

The Aztec priests performed an interesting ceremony to please Tlaloc. They threw themselves into lakes at midnight and imitated the sound of water birds to the point of exhaustion!

The Corn God

Corn was an important commodity in Aztec life and a symbol for life itself. Aztecs believed that human beings were made of bones, the blood of Quetzalcoatl and corn. The Corn God, Centeotl and his counterpart Chicomecoatl were worshipped as Gods of Food and Produce. Humans were sacrificed in their honour to keep them happy.

Since corn was the staple food for the Aztecs, the Corn God was worshipped with great reverence

Religion and Customs

Like most cultures, we too worshipped our gods. We also performed many rituals to keep them happy.

Aztec Beliefs

Aztec religion and worship was based on many beliefs and myths. They believed in thirteen heavens and nine hells. They thought it was the way a person died that determined whether he would go to heaven or to the underworld. They also believed that the sun fought darkness every night and rose to save mankind and if blood was offered, it would be happy and rise everyday. All rituals followed a basic structure which included fasting, purification, offerings and sacrifice.

Part of Life

Aztec religion focused on the four aspects that were most important to their civilization: creation, rain, fertility and war. Each of these was looked over by a group of deities. The Aztecs performed elaborate rituals to serve the gods. Religious ceremonies were a part of their daily life. The rituals involved gifts of incense, food, birds, animals and human beings. They also held performances as part of their religious ceremonies.

The Mexico flag bears the symbol of a perched eagle with a serpent in its mouth

Places of Worship

Huge pyramid structures were built in the Aztec capital of Tenochtitlan. These pyramids had temples of gods perched on top. It was here that the priests performed rituals to serve the large pantheon of Aztec gods. The Aztecs also offered their prayers to the gods in small neighbourhood temples. Attached to these places of worship were courts for ball games (*tlachtli*), sacrificial stones (*techcatl*) and many other special areas for ceremonies. Every ritual followed a basic structure that consisted of fasting, purification, offerings and sacrifice.

The Pyramid of the Sun where gods were worshipped by priests

Would you believe?

No other culture has offered so many humans as religious sacrifices as the Aztecs. It is thought that over 20,000 people were sacrificed annually!

Men for the Gods?

Aztecs believed that after the world had been destroyed four times in the past, many gods sacrificed themselves to recreate the world. Therefore, the Aztecs sacrificed humans as part of their religious rituals to repay the blood debt to the gods. Aztecs also believed the hearts and blood of humans to be the supreme offering for the gods, which would keep them happy. So they sacrificed humans for rain, for good crops, to avoid natural disasters and to win wars. Sometimes people offered themselves as sacrifice and at other times criminals, prisoners of wars and slaves were killed to please the gods. A common method of sacrifice was to cut open the chest with an obsidian knife and tear out the heart. Other methods included killing the victim with arrows or spears.

An Aztec man being sacrificed for the gods

Entertainment

We had many ways of enjoying ourselves. We played games, listened to music and danced at feasts and festivals.

Is it Basketball?

Games were played for fun but also served as rituals. One of the most popular games was the *tlachtli*. It was played between two teams using a rubber ball in an I-shaped court. The idea was to shoot the ball into the iron hoop placed on opposite walls at the end of the court. The players had to hit the ball using their hips, knees and elbows and were not allowed to use their hands or feet. The team that made the first "basket" won the game. Every Aztec city had a walled court near the temples for this sacred game.

Time to Gamble

Patolli was a popular gambling game. It was played with pebbles and dry beans on a X shaped board. The players rolled five beans which had white dots painted on them and were used as dice. The player had to move on the squares on the board according to the number on his beans. The first person to travel across the board and return home was the winner. Macuilxochitl was known as the deity of gambling, games, music and dance. The players invoked Macuilxochitl and offered him incense and food before starting a game of *patolli*.

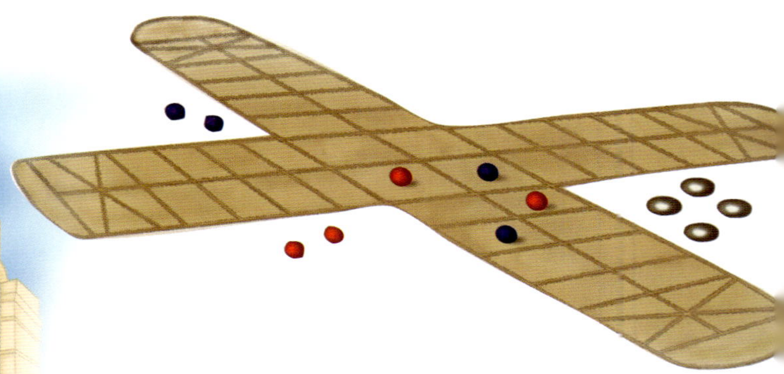

▲The name of the game *patolli* was derived from the Aztec word for bean - *patolli*, meaning fava or kidney beans

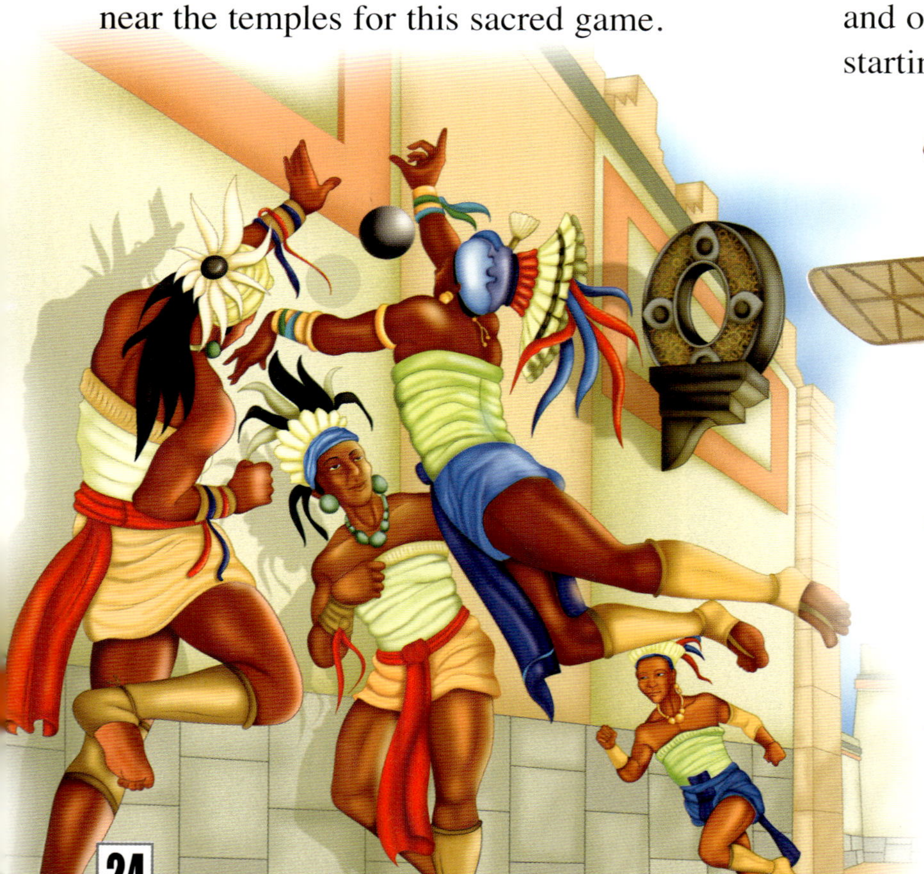

◄Popular games like basketball and other ball games have been developed from the ancient Aztec game of *tlachtli*

▲ Percussion instruments and trumpets were used to produce specific sounds and tunes

Would you believe?

It has been recorded that Moctezuma II and Cortes played totoloque together. Totoloque was a gambling game using pellets made of gold. They were allowed five attempts in which they gained or lost gold or jewels that they staked.

Dancing to the Tune

In the Aztec culture, both dance and music were closely related to religion and were a part of rites and rituals. The Aztecs danced, sang and played music to appease the gods. The ritual dance was known as *macehualiztli* and the popular dance was called *netotiliztli*. Their dances were like plays and described some story or myth. They also showed a relation between man and his world. While scudding and whirling steps showed fertility, some represented the earth and crops. The steps - that moved back and forth - represented fire, the zigzag ones symbolised water, while the spinning movements represented the soul.

What is That Music?

Music was a significant part of Aztec life. Aztec children were taught to play musical instruments, and to sing and dance. The musical instruments commonly used were rattles, whistles, trumpets, flutes, copper bells and shells. The big temple drums could be heard for several kilometres. The wind instruments of the Aztecs included pan pipes, whistles and flutes. In addition to this, dancers tied dried seeds on their feet for rhythmic sounds. Everyone had to learn music, songs and dances for festivals. Children between the age of 12 and 15 were sent to the *Cuicacalli* - also known as the House of Song - to learn these arts.

Aztec boys were taught basic domestic tasks, like fishing, by their parents

Education

We were especially interested in education. Our children were educated from a young age. They were not only taught by their parents at home but also went to school.

Learning at Home

The children received their first education at home from their parents, supervised by the authorities of their *calpulli*. Children were raised with care, ensuring that they knew their responsibilities and necessary life skills. Children also learnt the *huehuetlatolli* or the "words of the old ones". The parents also punished the children if they misbehaved. The most common punishment was to make the child inhale burning red chilli fumes.

School for Nobility

The children of nobility were sent to the *calmecac* which was the training ground for new military and religious leaders. The boys and girls were sent to different *calmecacs*. The schools were run by priests who taught various religious and administrative services. The children were given lessons in history, astronomy, poetry and writing. Warriors also taught the boys to fight in a battle. They were taken to a battle and shown how to take a prisoner captive.

Education for Girls

Aztec girls were mainly taught at home. While the boys received training from their fathers, the girls were taught by their mothers. Initially, the girls watched their mothers spin thread and cook. The girls usually began spinning at the age of six and cooking at the age of twelve. Their education was a training for marriage and housekeeping. The only school the Aztec girls attended was the House of Song where they were taught music, song and dance between the age of twelve and fifteen.

An Aztec woman teaching her daughter one of the basic duties of cooking

School for the Commoners

After receiving basic guidance from parents, the children of the commoners attended a school called the *tepochcalli*. There was a *tepochcalli* in each neighbourhood. Here the boys were taught basic occupational skills, like the elements of warfare and skills for good citizenship. At the age of fifteen the boys were sent to either a *calmecac*, if they were bright enough, or *cuicacalli*, which was the military school.

Would you believe?

Some children of commoners who were bright and intelligent were sent to a calmecac where they would have more emphasis on scholarship and advanced careers. This gave the meritorious commoners a chance to improve their station and climb up the social hierarchy.

tree/forest
(quauitl)

teeth
(tlantli)

mountain
(tepetl)

stone
(tetl)

Writing and Books

We needed to learn to write so that we could maintain administrative, financial and legal records. We developed our own system of writing and used pictures instead of words.

Picture Writing

The Aztecs developed an unique system of rebus or "picture writing". They drew figures to represent a word or a phrase. These figures or symbols, known as glyphs, were picked up from daily life and were understood by all the educated Aztecs. First the outlines of figures were sketched in black and then colour was filled in. Red, blue, yellow and green were the basic colours that were used. Colours helped to distinguish between figures that looked very similar. Since all names were of a descriptive type, the Aztecs also used glyphs for personal names and proper nouns. Writing symbols were not placed in sequence like letters and words in a book, but placed to form a larger picture or a scene. So an Aztec manuscript was like a picture puzzle which required skill and practice.

▼ The various symbols, or glyphs, shown across these pages were used for writing by the Aztecs

rabbit
(teepeti)

Teepatepee

Tepetitlan

Quauhnauac

Tochtepecan

Tenochtitlan

jar of honey

dead body

Codices

The books that the Aztecs wrote were known as codices. Each book or codex consisted of a strip, 12 m (39 ft) long and 15 cm (6 in) broad. It was made of paper from the bark of the fig tree, maguey cloth or deer skin. It was folded in a zigzag way and the ends were glued to thin wooden strips. Each page was read from top to bottom. Codices from the pre-conquest Aztec culture are rare: some that have survived are the Codex Borbonicus that talks about the Aztec religious calendar; the Boturini Codex that narrates the story of the journey of wandering Aztecs to Tenochtitlan; and the Codex Mendoza that documents Aztec rulers and their rule. The most useful is the Florentine Codex composed between 1540 and 1585. This codex is a treasure-trove of information and talks about Aztec life and culture before the Spanish conquest.

Would you believe?

Aztecs used symbols to also show numbers. The numbers 1-19 were shown by dots. They counted in multiples of 20. A flag represented the number 20, a feather stood for 400, while a pouch represented the number 8000.

This is a page from an original Aztec codice showing a human sacrifice

flint knife (teepeti)

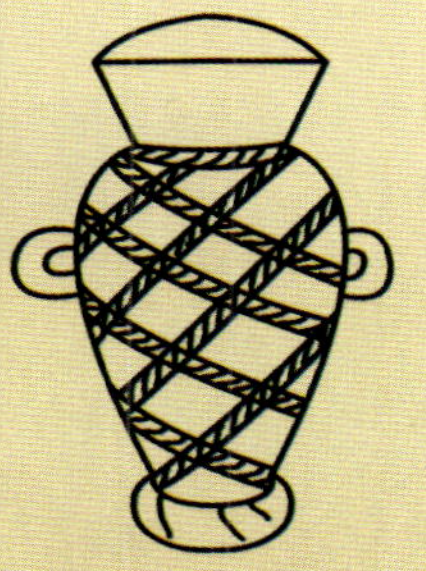

war

Calendars

Our priests were quite brilliant. They made two calendars — one to measure time and the other to fix religious ceremonies.

The Sacred Calendar

Apart from the 365 days calendar, the Aztec priests also designed a religious calendar. This ritual calendar had a 260 day cycle called *tonalpohualli*. Both the calendars ran together and the same day in each calendar fell at the same time once every 52 years. Thus, Aztec time was divided into 52-year cycles, just like our current 100 year cycles called centuries. The religious calendar was used for consulting the gods. Different days and months belonged to different gods. Children were sacrificed to please the water gods. On the five unlucky days no rituals were held and they were days of general fasting.

Quite Like Ours

The Aztecs used the time-measuring calendar to conduct their daily business and fix the best time to plant crops. This calendar had a 365 day cycle called *xiuhpohualli*. A year was divided into 18 months consisting of 20 days each. Every month had a name, and the days of the month were numbered from one to twenty. Each of the twenty days was shown by a different symbol. The days of the last month, Nemontemi, were numbered from one to five. These five days were considered inauspicious. It was believed that disasters would happen during these days.

▼ These symbols were used to depict the different days in a month

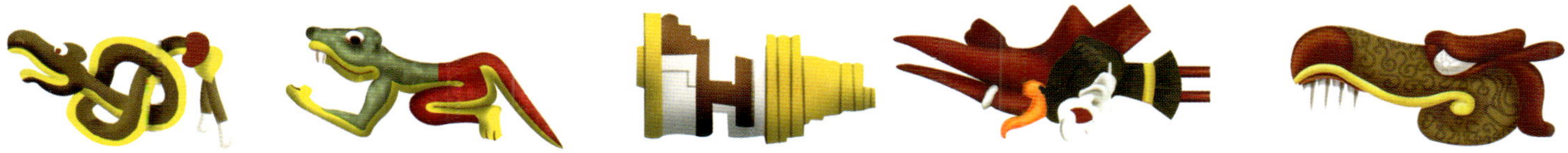

The Aztec Sun Stone

The Aztec calendar is recorded as a carving on the Aztec Sun Stone (sometimes mistakenly called the Aztec Calendar Stone) currently in the National Museum of Anthropology and History in Mexico City. This was known as *Cuauhxicalli* or the Eagle Bowl. It was carved and dedicated to the principal Aztec deity, the Sun. It weighs almost 25 tons, has a diameter of just under 3.5 m (12 ft), and a thickness of 1 m (3 ft). The centre of the disc has the face of the Sun God. The first ring from the centre shows the Four Olins representing the four Aztec epochs. The second ring consists of the signs for the 20 days of the month. The third ring shows the sun's rays that were meant to symbolise splashed blood or sacrifice. The outer ring shows a number of symbols like herbs, flames and Xiucoatl's tail.

Would you believe?

The 52-year cycle that marked the Aztec "century" was celebrated with great joy. There was a 12-day festival known as the New Fire Ceremony. People observed general fasting and put out lights for 12 days. On the midnight of the 12th day the priest would remove the heart of a victim and replace it with a piece of wood. Then this wood would be lit. Thus the new fire would once again light the city.

The Sun God depicted on the Sun Stone

Art & Architecture

We had many types of art and artists: some carved statues, some made feather head dresses and some made jewellery. Our architecture, especially the pyramids and temples, were examples of skill and genius.

The stone workers used simple tools made of wood, rock and bone to carve stone figures like these

Gold was used for making decorative pieces and ornaments

Of Crafts and Craftsmen

The Aztec society had all kinds of artisans and craftsmen. Stone workers carved statues, usually of gods, from rocks. They also made objects from very precious gems like jade, black obsidian and transparent crystals. The workers were trained from an early age and the skills they learnt were passed on from worker to worker. The potters made pots that were used for various purposes. The Aztec potters did not use the potter's wheel. Instead, they shaped clay with their hands. Feather workers made beautiful headdresses and garments for the noble families. Craftsmen who made gold and silver jewellery were probably the most important of all craft workers.

Would you believe?

The Aztec pyramids are a magnificent piece of architectural skill, especially considering, unlike the Egyptians, the Aztecs did not have wheels or pulleys to aid them in construction

Buildings to be Proud of

The Aztecs were skilled architects. Of all the buildings they made, the temples were the biggest and best decorated. The temples looked like the great Egyptian pyramids except that they did not have a pointed top. Aztec temples had a flat top and two small compartments where the sacrifices would be held. These pyramids usually had four stages, with platforms in between. The Aztecs always wanted to make sacrificial temples to please their gods but could not destroy the old ones. So they built new temples over the old ones! They made the new temples larger, more extravagant, and more pleasing to the eye with each new layer.

The pyramids had stairs on all four sides reaching upto the sacrificial temple on top

The Aztecs used feathers of tropical birds to make headdresses and garments

Cities and Roads

We had well planned cities that made life comfortable for us and the roads and canals helped with good transport and trade.

Well Planned Cities

When the Aztecs landed at Tenochtitlan they had difficulty living on the swamps. However, this hardy and strong race soon made best use of things to become prosperous. Most Aztec cities had a similar layout. Aztec cities were divided into different areas. At the centre of the city was the walled temple area. The rest of the city spread out from this holy place of worship and sacrifice. Among the other buildings were the royal palaces and homes of important nobles. Then there were the homes of the traders, the homes and workshops of artisans and homes of commoners. These were in different "wards" based on the *calpulli*. Each had its own school and marketplace. There was also the main market place where food, pots, precious stones, cloth, fuel, tools and animal skins were sold. The Aztecs built roads intersecting each other at 90°. The canals that interlaced the cities were used for transport. People travelled in flat-bottomed canoes from one place to another. The largest and most important Aztec city was Tenochtitlan. Built on Lake Texcoco, it was the capital city of the Aztecs. The city was destroyed in 1521 by the Spaniards. The new Mexico City was erected on top of its ruins.

Would you believe?

The Aztecs built their temples in the centre of their city. This is because the Aztecs had five directions: north, south, east, west, and centre. They believed that the centre was where the world joined the world of the gods and the different worlds they went to after death.

A diagram of the city of Tenochtitlan

Important buildings were carved and painted both on the outside and the inside
Temples were rebuilt over the old temples
These were paved roads and paved open spaces known as plazas

Trade and Traders

Trade, agriculture and manufacturing formed the base of our economy. Traders travelled between cities and to other empires and helped make our land prosperous and wealthy.

Rise of the Traders

As the kingdom of the Aztecs expanded it became difficult for the *calpulli* of one city to visit another city to exchange goods. So a class of travelling merchant traders, known as the *pochteca*, rose. They travelled through the empire and brought back exotic goods such as coloured feathers, jade and cocoa. They also brought back obsidian and bronze and sold their goods in the city markets. The marketplace was an important centre in Aztec cities. Gradually this class gained a firm hold in the social order and started gaining wealth. Soon they began to take on the mannerisms and privileges of the nobility.

Many Roles

The merchants were divided into many different categories and had several roles. The highest officials of the *pochteca* were the *pochtecatlatoque*. They were the seniors in the trade and no longer travelled. Slave traders formed an important sub-group of *pochteca*. They were known as *tlatlani* and were the richest merchants and most important people. A third group of long distance traders called *tencunenenque* worked for the rulers, carrying out trade for them. The last group, the *naualoztomeca*, were spies disguised as *travellera*. They brought back vital news and information.

Merchants travelled through the empire and brought back exotic goods

Beasts of Burden?

The Aztecs had no animals, wagons or vehicles for transporting their goods. The only mode of transport was the canoe, which could be used only in water. So what did they use on land? Porters or slaves were used to carry large amounts of goods from one place to another. Porters led a tough life carrying huge loads on their backs, with a strap around their forehead for support, from one city to another.

What is this Money?

Trade was considered to be an important part of the Aztec economy. The Aztecs did not have paper or metal money. But they did have a currency of cacao beans! Cacao beans, imported from lowland areas, were treated as a precious substance and were used in local markets to purchase things. While trading with other empires the Aztecs exchanged gold and jewellery for rare items like rubber and cotton and animal skin.

Would you believe?

Aztec commoners had to pay tribute or tax to the government. It could be paid in crops, cloth, and jewellery or by working in state projects like the building of temples etc. The Aztecs made most wealth by extracting tribute from subject tribes they conquered. Often, these tribes were forced to pay so much tribute that they lived on the brink of starvation.

▲ Cacao beans like these were used as currency by the Aztecs

► Pots made by artisans were sold in the marketplace

Warriors and Battles

Warriors were highly admired and valued in our society. Every able man was expected to wish to be a warrior and fight battles.

Reasons for Warfare

Warfare was the driving force behind the Aztec society. There were two main reasons for warfare: The first was, of course, political; they fought wars to establish their control over neighbouring lands; the second reason was religion. The sacrifice of war captives was a significant part of Aztec festivals. This was known as the *Xochiyaoyotl* or the Flowery Wars and were fought between smaller armies.

Honourable Warriors

All able bodied Aztec men were trained to be warriors. It was considered a duty and an honour. When a boy was born his umbilical cord was cut off, dried and buried on the battlefield to signify that his life would be dedicated to war. The Aztec army was divided into two layers. The commoners were organized into "wards" under the leadership of the *Tiachcahuan* and the *Calpoleque*. The nobles were organized into professional warrior societies. There was a High General known as the *Tlacochcalcatl* and a General known as the *Tlacateccatl*. The priests also took part in warfare and often carried effigies of gods to the battlefield.

The Flowery Wars were fought to capture prisoners as sacrificial victims for the gods

The Aztecs wore very colourful costumes for battle

Warrior Societies

Warriors who excelled in battles, capturing or killing large numbers, were placed in warrior societies. Chief among these were the Eagle and Jaguar societies. Warriors who belonged to these societies dressed up in feathers and the pelts of the respective creatures. It was a great honour to be able to wear these costumes. The most fierce of the societies was the society of the "Shorn Ones". Their heads were shaven bald except for a long braid over the left ear. They painted their head and face half blue and another half red or yellow. They were sworn never to turn back in battle.

Armour and Weapons

Aztec warriors wore elaborate costumes of their particular society during battles. Ordinary troops wore costumes decorated with patterns and emblems made from feather and leather. Shields were made either from wood or maize cane. They also wore thick quilted cotton armour that swords and spears had difficulty in penetrating. Their weapons included spears, wooden swords with obsidian blades, clubs, bow and arrows and stone slings.

Would you believe?

Warfare was driven by the expectations of the king to expand the kingdom. The first action of a ruler was to stage a military campaign to show his ability as a warrior. A failed coronation campaign was seen as an extremely bad omen for the rule of a Tlatoani.

Spanish Conquest

It was the "discovery" of America by Christopher Columbus in 1492 that inspired Hernan Cortes to sail to our continent for gold and to destroy us.

Why the Aztecs Fell

Aztecs were powerful warriors who were destroyed by just a handful of soldiers. Just before the Spanish explorer Hernan Cortes arrived, the Aztecs had seen several astrological phenomena, all of which seemed to signify Quetzalcoatl's imminent return to destroy the empire. Quetzalcoatl was thought to have light hair and complexion, and so Cortes was subsequently mistaken for him. Moreover, Cortes arrived at the time of harvest when the Aztecs were not at all ready for war. Cortes also combined the forces of other smaller empires against them. The outbreak of small pox also weakened the Aztecs and helped Cortes wipe them out!

The Destruction of Tenochtitlan

The Aztecs thought that Cortes was actually Quetzalcoatl who had come to destroy their empire. Moctezuma sent him gold and other gifts hoping that, pleased with the gifts, the Spaniards would leave the city without harming them. However, this only made the visitors greedy and they advanced towards the Aztec city of Tenochtitlan. Cortes and his men were received by Moctezuma II himself. The clever Cortes soon took Moctezuma II captive, hoping to rule through him. After the death of Moctezuma II the Aztecs, under the leadership of Cuitlahuac, attacked the Spaniards. The visitors fled, only to return with a better army. The Aztecs fought bravely but surrendered after 80 days of battle.

The Aztecs believed that Quetzalcoatl would destroy their empire

Consequences of the Conquest

After the conquest there was an exchange of Aztec and Spanish cultures. Many of the Aztec nobility learnt Spanish and Spanish missionaries learnt and wrote about Aztec culture. However, the Spanish officers exploited the Aztecs and made them work as labourers. They also forced the Aztecs to adopt Christianity. Aztec priests were killed and the temples and statues of gods were destroyed. Their codices were destroyed and they were forbidden to learn about their own culture. They were also forced to read and write in Spanish.

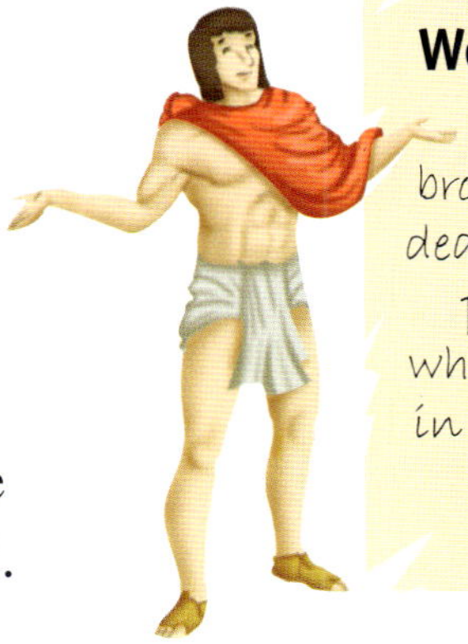

Would you believe?

The Spanish had brought with them two deadly diseases - small pox and measles - which killed thousands in the Aztec kingdom.

Moctezuma II offered Cortes all the gold and riches in his kingdom

Timeline

c. 1100	Aztecs leave homeland in search of new home
1195	Aztecs arrive in the Valley of Mexico
c. 1250	Aztecs settle in swamps near Lake Texcoco
1325	Tenochtitlan is founded; First temple is built by Aztecs
c. 1350	Causeways built with canals
1370	Tenoch, Aztec Priest-Ruler, dies
1375	Acamapichtli becomes first king of Aztecs
1397	Huitzilihuitl is elected the second ruler
c. 1400	Aztecs expand and rule whole valley
1417	Chimalpopoca is the new ruler
1428	Itzcoatl becomes new ruler; Joins forces with Texcoco and Tlacopan to form Triple Alliance; Atzcapotzalco is conquered
1440	Moctezuma I begins his rule
1452	Tenochtitlan is destroyed by flood
1452-4	Famine in the kingdom
1455	Moctezuma begins mass sacrifices

1469 Moctezuma I dies; Axayacatl is the new king

1481 Tizoc is the new ruler; He is quite weak and cowardly

1486 Ahuizotu becomes the new ruler

1487 The Great Temple is built at Tenochtitlan; Aztecs expand southward into Mayan territories

1502 Moctezuma II becomes the ruler; Aztec Empire is at its height

1519 Cortez, the Spanish Conquerer, comes to Mexico; Moctezuma II killed

1520 Cuitlahuac elected ruler

1521 Tenochtitlan destroyed by Spaniards

1522 Tenochtitlan rebuilt, named Mexico City; It is declared the capital of Spanish colony of New Spain

Glossary

Agriculture: The art of growing crops

Appease: To satisfy

Assess: To estimate the value of something

Astronomy: The scientific study of stars and planets

Codex: A manuscript

Confiscation: To sieze something

Economy: Financial activity in a country or region

Effigy: A figure or dummy of a person

Extravagant: Something more than the ordinary

Fraud: Deception or trickery

Glyph: A symbolic figure

Inauspicious: Unlucky

Incense: Perfumed sticks used in festivals

Interlaced: To interweave

Imminent: About to occur

Loincloth: A single piece of cloth worn around the waist, generally by males

Meritorious: Exceptionally talented

Midwives: Women trained to assist in childbirth

Obsidian: Black, hard volcanic glass

Pantheon: All gods considered as a group

Portent: A sign of something important about to occur

Pragmatic: Practical

Revered: Honoured or worshipped

Resurrected: To be brought back to life

Retrieve: To get back again

Soothsayer: One who is able to predict events

Index